THE WORLD THAT THE SHOOTER LEFT US

Cyrus Cassells

Four Way Books
Tribeca

Library of Congress Cataloging-in-Publication Data

Names: Cassells, Cyrus, author.
Title: The world that the shooter left us / Cyrus Cassells.
Description: [New York] : Four Way Books, [2022] | Identifiers: LCCN 2021045639 |
ISBN 9781954245099 (trade paperback) |
ISBN 9781954245174 (epub)
Subjects: LCGFT: Poetry.
Classification: LCC PS3553.A7955 W67 2022 | DDC 811/.54--dc23
LC record available at https://lccn.loc.gov/2021045639

This book is manufactured in the United States of America and printed on
acid-free paper.

Four Way Books is a not-for-profit literary press. We are grateful for the assistance
we receive from individual donors, public arts agencies, and private foundations
including the NEA, NEA Cares, Literary Arts Emergency Fund, and the
New York State Council on the Arts, a state agency.

We are a proud member of the Community of Literary Magazines and Presses.

THE WORLD THAT THE SHOOTER LEFT US

Also by Cyrus Cassells

Poetry

The Mud Actor
Soul Make a Path through Shouting
Beautiful Signor
More Than Peace and Cypresses
The Crossed-Out Swastika
The Gospel according to Wild Indigo
More Than Watchmen at Daybreak

Translations

Still Life with Children: Selected Poems of Francesc Parcerisas

CONTENTS

I. The World That the Shooter Left Us

The World That the Shooter Left Us 3
Sin Eater, Beware 6
Ready! Aim! Fire! 9
Election 11
Is Not (Don't Interrupt the Sorrow) 13
My Black Friend 17
Plantation Tour (One Star!) 19
Dosage 20
The Spirits of Slave Catchers Are Still Walking Among Us 23

II. Boys Don't Do That to Other Boys

Here, Sir Fire! 27
Boys Don't Do That to Other Boys 29
Trafficked Angel 38
The Mother Who Says Yes to the Sword 45
The GB Brothers Strike Again 47
Me Too, Me Too 48

III. Harum-Scarum

Finding America in Goya's "Black Paintings" 57
Like Christ Overturning the Moneylenders' Tables 59
Senator, Where is Your Voodoo Doll, Your Snare? 61
The Absence of the Witch Does Not Invalidate the Spell 63
Quid Pro Quo (Two Baritones on a Phone) 65
Harum-Scarum Photo Op 68
The Hood 70
The Only Way To Fight the Plague is Decency 72

IV. Tango With a Ghost

Obliterate Asylum!   77
Requiem for Óscar and Valeria: The Crossing   79
Martín Getsemany, I See You   81
Clarinet   83
Tango with a Ghost   86
    I. Buenos Aires Overture
    II. The Living Room Gasp
    III. The Vanishing & the Roaring
    IV. Tango with a Ghost
Icebox   94
    I. To the Gladiator in the Rogue Arena
    II. Those "Return to Senders" Children
    III. Icebox
    IV. The Smithsonian Considers Purchasing the Art
       of Formerly Detained Children
    V. Flu Boy Motionless in a Pool
    VI. A Toddler's Day in Court
Courage Song for Scott Warren   102

This book is for Edward Garza, with great love and admiration, and for Suzanne Gardinier, *Hermana*

AND NOW

And now as you read these poems
—you whose eyes and hands I love
—you whose mouth and eyes I love
—you whose words and minds I love—
don't think I was trying to state a case
or construct a scenery:
I tried to listen to
the public voice of our time
tried to survey our public space
as best I could
—tried to remember and stay
faithful to details, note
precisely how the air moved
and where the clock's hands stood
and who was in charge of definitions
and who stood by receiving them
when the name of compassion
was changed to the name of guilt
when to feel with a human stranger
was declared obsolete.

Adrienne Rich

I. THE WORLD THAT THE SHOOTER LEFT US

THE WORLD THAT THE SHOOTER LEFT US

in memory of J. Garza, 1949-2017

In this one, ladies and gentlemen,
Beware, be clear: the brown man,

The able lawyer, the paterfamilias,
Never makes it out of the poem alive:

The rash, all-too-daily report,
The out-of-the-blue bullet

Blithely shatters our treasured
Legal eagle's bones and flesh—

In the brusque spectacle of point-blank force,
On a crimsoned street,

Where a revered immigrant plummets
Over a contested parking spot,

And the far-seeing sages insist,
Amid strident maenads

Of breakneck patrol car sirens,
Clockwork salvos,

The charismatic Latino lawyer's soul
Is banished, elsewhere, without a shred

Of eloquence in the matter—
And the brute, churning

Surfaces of the world,
They bear our beloved citizen away—

Which means, austere saints
And all-seeing masters,

If I grasp your bracing challenge:
At our lives' most brackish hour,

Our highest mission isn't just to bawl,
But to turn the soul-shaking planet

Of the desecrated parking lot
(The anti-miracle),

The blunt, vitriolic white man's
Unnecessary weapon,

And the ruse of self-defense
Into justice-cries and ballots?

Into newfound pledges,
And particles of light?

SIN-EATER, BEWARE

So you're intent on devouring the sins
Of the plundering country

That murdered your pedestrian sons,
Your seldom-cop-safe children,

That tore the defiant music
From your paragon chest, the inmost

Prayer from your winter-cracked
Yet rancor-less lips—

Exorcist, it won't be easy!
Sin-eater, would-be saint, beware!

For breakfast: genocide, buffalo hides,
Broadcast feathers & scattered

Wampum beads—
For lunch: bustling cotton gins,

An overseer's rusted iron "bit,"
Egregious auction blocks,

Baleful phantoms of merciless slave ships still
Docking on these bartering shores...

At dinnertime, scarring billyclubs,
Brass-knuckled rent-a-thugs

& fearsome strike-breakers,
Atomic clouds, open-air assassinations,

Baptist church burnings & syphilis "trials"
On unsuspecting Black recruits—

For (almost superfluous) dessert:
Abetting, love-it-or-leave-it senators,

Pillaged or shuttered abortion clinics,
Tiki Torches & staining swastikas—

Yes, dauntless, sin-eliminating Hercules,
Be sure never to relinquish

The raise-the-roof tools
Of your holy warrior's arsenal:

A colossal, never-ending platter,
A fleet (albeit figurative) deveining knife

& a formidable, Gulliver-sized fork—
Not to mention,

An arch, invisible bulldozer
& an immense matching bib,

A massive, hardworking syphon
For your hallowing, absolving mouth

& of course, a seamless heart
Like Mother Mary's,

For the benighted seasons
When our hate-laden republic implodes...

READY! AIM! FIRE!

In the *Ready! Aim! Fire!* of the new
Indignant, open-carry era

(Blood stains on the salient leaves & branches
Of the Tree of Life),

Corinna emphasizes: in protean English
We have a plethora of words

For lethal weapons & of course,
Columbine, Sandy Hook & Parkland

Aren't the three names of coruscating,
Stop-the-presses! Graces.

Rabbi Lev confesses that he must now post
A chilling sign proclaiming

Firearms aren't allowed
In synagogue pews

Or anywhere near the Torah scrolls;
Yes, in tabernacles

& doleful churches,
In wailing school parking lots, we cry

We can't go on living like this
& then we go on living like this:

Deadfall, savage protocol
Splattered all over our classrooms.

ELECTION

On the noisome morning
Of the tampered election, we found

Posters eclipsing university buildings,
Inglorious flyers

Soliciting arrest & torture,
Tar & feathering—

Meant to gag
"Left-leaning campus leaders"—

Flash! Timber!
In ignoble fall, we woke

To a flinty, fist-&-bicep era:
Defiled headstones,

Daily alarums of mordant threats
Aimed at impassive elders,

Passersby jostled on municipal streets—
We woke to

Reptile-cool comets of spit,
Unremitting slurs

& Muslim girls taunted & slapped
On public buses,

Non compos mentis for a king,
Flimflam, an unbridled foundry

Of chicanery, a crafty corsair's
Or a vehement robber baron's

Loot-fast dynasty.
Yes, we woke, incredulous,

To dewy-faced fifth graders
Lowering deliberately

In a sun-flecked field
To fashion a human swastika—

IS NOT (DON'T INTERRUPT THE SORROW)

in memory of Eric Garner, 1970-2014

A Taser is not an answer
A rushing bullet is not a dream

There is no sunny god
In an Apollo Helmet

A livelong mercenary is not
A frisking meadow lamb

Lady Justice is no
Fearsome chimera

No lurking drone
No business-as-usual Cerberus

A callous Caesar is not
A far-seeing Christ—

*

Listen: a blazing Mississippi cross
Never presages a messiah.

A daffodil in a "sundown town" never signals
The onset of spring—

*

So after two callous seasons,
I finally dared to inquire

If his taken-too-soon father's ousting
"Stand Your Ground" assassin

Was indeed white, "lily-white"
& naturally his response

In this volatile demesne,
This gallery of averted eyes

& gimcrack defenders galore
Was yes

Dear God of course yes

*

Don't interrupt the sorrow
A woman croons

But all I catch is the *ack-ack-ack*
Of ink-blotter redaction,

The X-rated sputter of a black site's
Water-boarded man

Or a flailing cigarette seller,
Cuffed, gasping for air,

Jinxing arm & insignia
Marring his throat:

Is not

Is not

Is not

Is not—

MY BLACK FRIEND

is dark-hued as Mississippi Delta Blues,
Black as a chain gang at nightfall.

He's cool; he's no fist-raised radical.
It's no heavy bead of sweat, I swear,

If I touch his nappy hair
Or blunder & use the N word.

I could even whistle "Dixie"
& I'm sure my boy Leroy

Wouldn't bat an eye.
Despite the full-time mumbo jumbo

About Ebony vs. Ivory clashes, fisticuffs,
Myself, I don't really see color:

My handy-dandy friend ensures
I'm never mistaken for a holdover,

A vile antebellum auctioneer
Or an ultra-bigot like Archie Bunker.

After my platonic praise session,
My minstrel-cool Song of Songs

(He's dark-skinned but comely,
Black as a desert tent in Kedar

Or a caliph's midnight sash),
Delicate snowflake,

Did you suspect my scaredy-cat ace of spades
Already? Oh, hipper-than-thou,

Liberal-or-less Mata Hari, I surrender!:
My Stepin Fetchit friend

Is blunt as a coal-black Baptist bier.
Yes, he's lead-riddled & cadaver-still

Like that cornered little flirt Emmett Till.

PLANTATION TOUR (ONE STAR!)

"Vacationers have been sharing their disdain
for guides emphasizing the annals of slavery."

What I didn't need, let me tell you,
Cher Guilt-Instilling Know-it-all,

Was a boring-as-sawdust lecture at Belle Fleur
About the bone-breaking perils of slavery!

FYI, Miss Firebrand Liberal,
It wasn't all that bad: I've heard

Plantation slaves often sang happily
While collecting cotton—

Look, I can't possibly be racist because
I'm Sicilian-American: see?

My people never enslaved anybody!

DOSAGE

Since you ask,
It's always a firehosing summer

In the unrelenting Dixie
Of the antebellum mind

(Bell as in belligerent!):
Drawn, not quite rusted swords,

Cobwebbed oaths
& querulous cannon-fire

Of the intractable Confederacy,
Smudged postcards from the plantation

Picnic-cum-lynching,
Punishing stars & barricading stripes

Arriving as a plebeian barrage
Of handcuffs, rubber bullets

& cop-lobbed canisters of tear gas—
Open wide!

Here's your daily dosage
Of breathlessness & Black body counts,

Rakish chokeholds
& blue-serge knees to the neck—

Which only the Dashcams' upbraiding oracles
Bother to reveal—

Speaking of can-do doses & cure-alls,
Folks, there's a deadsure virus

On the loose,
So what's the perfect ratio

Between household cleaner
& human blood?

The right-as-rain
(Or heaven-sent manna) dose

Of "controversial" hydroxychloroquine?
Shorty the never-fail bootlegger insists

It's all about mixing the moonshine,
The backwoods hooch just right

Without killing the clients!
The secret's in the sauce...

Admits one repentant Dixie belle
After viewing the inglorious footage:

I do declare,
When poor, luckless Mr. Floyd

Cried out for his mama,
It broke my barbecue & hush puppy heart!

It broke the camel's back,
O my country-'tis-of-thee—

THE SPIRITS OF SLAVE CATCHERS ARE STILL WALKING AMONG US

Full frontal blast of the N word
Sullying the windshield of your family car,

Or sprayed on your innocuous
Chapel door—

See, the spirits of slave catchers are still
Hectoring, ensnaring:

Unerring bloodhounds on the track...
At the mall esplanade,

In the glittering bean-shaped pool,
At the mild-as-milk library story hour:

Where is your pass?
Brash, unfailing hunters

Trailing your workaday step:
Tireless collaborators,

Quick-to-call Beckys & Karens,
Tattletale belles all too avid to sip

From Whites Only fountains once more—
Restless enforcers insisting

Black bodies stay ghetto-bound, earthbound,
Cradle-still in velvet-lined

Elm or alder wood coffins—
Sundown towns, they're labeled,

Because: "Lord, you can't be Black after dark
& expect to make it out alive!"—

Say it with me: dull & cavalier
As a delta-bound train's Jim Crow curtain,

The spirits of restless slave-catchers are still
Roaming among us,

Hungering, unceasing,
The spirits of slave catchers are still...

II. BOYS DON'T DO THAT TO OTHER BOYS

HERE, SIR FIRE!

after Picasso's drawing Caballo Corneado

Lamp-black,
The shadow of my mane on fire.

My unstinting hooves,
My breakneck soul insisted

I could be masterless,
Free of reins.

But now, impinging king,
Agile arsonist, your once-allaying

Song of protection
Has been unmasked

As a match-flare, a hunter's snare,
A burning meadow—

Surprise!
A disavowing,

An armed & quisling fist
Thrusts up

Through the beleaguered topsoil,
The blackened grasses

& only blood wells
From the oracular guitar—

No more blandishments, no more
Pious disguises:

Dissembler, betrayer,
Flame & conquering knife, it's you.

It's you who've come
To pierce my point-blank belly—

BOYS DON'T DO THAT TO OTHER BOYS

What is it about passed-out cold
That you find so sexy?

*

I didn't say you could put your hands
I didn't say could put your hands on me without my

*

Rape? I'd be super-careful
About that label!

The truth is, little bitch,
You texted me;

You asked for it,
So why all the boo-hoo suddenly?

*

At the Captain's Xmas Party
(Where the main goal's just

Tequila shots, mistletoe & losing
Your totally annoying cherry),

Man, after a little while,
I could barely move an inch,

Much less yell *stop!*
I swear, for sure, Mr. Sexy Sneak,

You slipped me
A roofie or somesuch

& let a few of the big-ass dudes on the team...
You kept shoving drinks

Down my sophomore throat:
Don't be shy, little guy,

You coaxed,
You're one of us now!

Next thing I know I wake up
With slashed jeans at my ankles,

Hot pink lipstick
Smeared on my lips,

Pain in my ass
& a mighty suspicious-looking

Broom nearby,
With ugly photos of it all

Blasted on the Internet & tagged:
"Pretty Party Trash!"

*

Of course I was expelled
& had a shitload of explaining to do

To my freaked-out,
Now totally former girlfriend

(Whom I actually love!)
& my single Mom,

Who didn't have an inkling
About Little Sonny Boy's secret side:

About my guy-on-guy curiosity
& hardcore hook-up sites

Or my half-baked desire
To try a bit of choking—

I was already mega-guilty
About the sexy older dudes on Grindr

Who didn't seem to give a _____
Whether I was underage:

Kiddo, what r u in 2?
Pitch? Catch?

Do u like it ruff?
Gotta wife, a 2-year-old at home

But just need to be my honest to God self
Sometimes, u know?

Son, u r really pretty—
Ha ha! "Pretty party trash!"

*

At first, your Bible-toting Mom protested
Boys don't do that to other boys!

But then nifty detectives found
Traces of your jizz on my shorts,

So you tried an Irish goodbye
With a serious mess of pills,

Since not a single soul
At Grayson High suspected

Our Handsome All-Star Athlete
& Future Class Valedictorian

Might be a closet gay:
You're *that* good of an actor—

Your highfalutin' Mom
Paid a pissed-off visit

To my Mom's mini-grocery store:
I saw those twisted texts!

Let me say it plain: your son's
A stone cold whore!—

Latrice Jamison,
Have you lost your mind?

Please leave my store right now.
You're frightening my customers!

Lady, I'm warning you!
Drop the charge!

*

When the salty texts between us
Went hella-public, most town folks

Tagged it as consensual,
But you & I know better, don't we?—

Meanwhile, "as the world turns,"
Your little holy-roller brother sprays

GOD HATES FAGS in screaming black
On the high school cafeteria walls

& lands his sorry ass in detention,
As the whole friggin' town gossips & unravels

Over my "inconvenient truth,"
Somehow, in the midst of it all,

Surprise! I've got a jock boyfriend:
Imagine, when Jed trailed me

Into the school john
(I was desperate for a smoke!)

I was sure he planned to slap me
Or even beat me up,

But lo & behold,
He actually French-kissed me instead—

God, I love him to pieces
But even *he* doesn't get

Why I'm still a sure-enough slave
To these awful party flashbacks:

Dude, with all the love I'm givin' you,
Are you still worked up

About some 2AM hook-up gone bad?
He's buff & way bigger than me,

So he doesn't have a clue
What it's like to be dissed or overpowered—

My stupid-as-a-clown hometown
Keeps attacking me & Mom 24/7

(Christ! No way she deserves this!)
But in spite of it all—

The whole Mothra vs. Godzilla train wreck
& my need to maybe transfer

To a not-so-wigged-out school,
I'm still proud of the moment

When I had the balls to call:
Officer, I'd like to report a rape...

TRAFFICKED ANGEL

When I finally opened my mouth to reveal
I'd been a teenage slave,

A crooning altar boy for sale,
Like a tender nightingale stuffed in a cage—

Nothing came out for a while
But a long mournful E.

Sad to say, my singing chops weren't enough
To save me from the nonstop

"Misery, meet your husband, Gloom"
Of a shoes-without-laces foster home,

That's where Virgilio, or "Jefe"
(As I learned to call him) stepped in:

When it comes to Boy Wonder's talent,
Hey, the sky's the limit!

Sure shot, I'll manage him & become
The baby songbird's pal & guardian—

For about a year,
V. was patient as can be, providing

Savvy insider tips about the business
& top-notch music lessons.

Then one day he summoned me
An hour before our regular rehearsal

& suddenly asked to kiss
My sockless & defenseless feet:

Don't worry, kid, this is normal,
But we'll need to keep

My little worship of your twinkle toes
A secret—

In no time flat, he groomed me
To service a gallery of older men:

CEOs, priests, celebrities...
Baby, think of it as leche

Or a scoop of the Häagen-Dazs
You like to scarf down so much.

Mijo, *stop blubbering*
& learn to love it, like I do!

When he wasn't "relishing" my toes
& telling his pervy circle

Of high-paying johns
Who purchased me,

90% of them "shrimp queens":
"Fernan's got the voice, the lips & feet

Of a perfect angel!
Who wants to start the bidding?"—

Sometimes, fueled with pricey Columbian,
A snowstorm of coke

Or big swigs of Demerara rum,
Jefe would cry & apologize

For all the ____ he was doing to me.
To salve his sorry conscience, I suppose,

He'd book a few four- & five-star gigs,
Then boast: *With his unmistakable voice,*

Fernan's one of God's sweetest angels;
I tell you, he's like my very own son.

Sometimes, damn him, behind closed doors,
He actually billed the two of us as

"A sexy real-life father & son,
Jefe & Efe,"

So the customers could get off
On the whole, eye-popping incest thing—

When I finally broke down & confessed
To my sweet rock of a music coach

That for almost four years
Jefe had been pimping me out,

Nicanor actually wept & urged me:
Nando, you better call the cops

& get the hell away from
Your effing Svengali!"

Virgilio's crocodile tears & bluffing threats
(To blackmail my deadbeat,

Long out-of-the-picture dad
& land his no-count ass back in jail)

Couldn't put a halt to my getaway plan;
Think on it: what card-carrying perp

Or shifty-eyed pedophile
Ever fesses up to anything?

The *pendejos* go on denying
Their filthy deeds till the end.

Charged with rape & human trafficking,
Now Mr. Badass Jefe claims

We were "for better or worse, engaged
In a hearts-&-flowers romance,"

Insists he's got letters,
Secret valentine snapshots proving

"We just couldn't keep our hands
Off each other,"

Evidence that I'm just testy, bitter,
Dead set on revenge—

Like the "hell hath no fury"
Villainess of my beloved *telenovela*

Or a fed-up Frida Kahlo on the warpath,
Lashing out at cheating Diego.

Dear fans, of course, I'm relieved
& over the pumpkin-fat moon to be free of

My sicko show biz slave-master,
But, of course, I'll never rest completely

Till my teen-loving Virgilio
Festers behind bars:

Yes, my invisible wings are intact,
My worshipped angel feet

Are on solid-as-Gibraltar ground
& when I belt out a song nowadays, you hear

The whole truth burning in my voice.

THE MOTHER WHO SAYS YES
TO THE SWORD

O has-been mother of the free-flowing booze
& handy diet pills,

You cashed me in—a cool sacrifice: to jump-
Start your floundering career,

You let the bozo Lothario
You got hitched to

Turn me into his very own
Beverly Hills 90210 Pinocchio,

While Ms. Pampered As F___ Actress was oh-so-busy
Elsewhere: sloshed, passed out

On Tarantino's set, or tanning
In some posh Emerald Coast location.

When the subject turned to
Your eldest son's welfare, you flat-out lied

To the drooling media,
On your coke-nosed Geppetto's behalf,

But my adorable, Clearasil nose
Never grew an inch in the courtroom—

Mama, on the witness stand,
You're like the cagey shrike

Gauging King Solomon's testing sword,
The lowdown, biblical fake,

Who, in order to stake
Her maternal claim,

Doesn't hesitate to agree
To sever her young son's body—

THE GB BROTHERS STRIKE AGAIN

Baby boy recruit, I guess you know by now
What the GB stands for:

Captured ass, lips & tits
Under our command!—

Are we not men & conquerors?

ME TOO, ME TOO

Between you & me,
I had a helluva lot of kissing practice in 3rd grade

With my gymnast babysitter
(He was an ace at the rings & side horse!)

& I guess I thought
I was more or less his boyfriend

(It was sorta romantic
Since he never _____ me),

So, when all the moony high school girls
Sighed in his Superman wake,

I felt a kept-quiet pride
That I probably knew

His award-winning varsity body,
His sensuous lips & busy-as-hell tongue,

Better than they did!
I recalled all this

When my co-worker Gina
Claimed our ridiculously amorous

& hairy-chested boss
Exposed himself to her at lunch break:

Cy, he's so good-looking,
You know for a minute, just a minute,

After the initial shock,
I thought of humoring his randy ass,

As if I were in some kind of Playgirl *fantasy*
Then I decided I'd rather cut off his _____.

A few days later, in solidarity, I confide:
Gina, once upon a time,

I thought I'd nailed the part,
My film break was finally in sight—

When the leering director queried,
Are you willing to go down under?

Excuse me, I asked, *will we be*
Shooting in Australia?

Cute! Quick-witted,
I like that!

& then there was the time
I was a Summer Abroad student

& a Brit expat prof invited me
To his fancy-pants country home;

When I got off the bus in some quaint Tuscan town,
He whispered straightaway:

My young thespian, we are *going to make love,*
Aren't *we?* I was 100% startled

But didn't miss a beat: *no, professor,*
I believe you invited me to lunch!

Two hours passed, slow as molasses
& Lord So-and-So was still

Pressuring me big time for sex,
So I insisted he put me

On the 3PM regional bus
All the way back to Florence

& of course, wouldn't you know?
I never even got lunch!

I had a weakling moment
When a little pitchfork voice went off:

Cy, he's plenty rich & not bad looking,
What's the big deal?

That's when I realized
That doe-fast urge to surrender

Was the 3rd-grader in me
Who didn't have a choice,

That Mr. Side Horse
With his hot, pleasing mouth

& mighty wrists,
His washboard stomach & outsized _____,

Wasn't my boyfriend,
God help me, but my abuser...

Gina laments,
I'm a gazillion percent sure

This is Mr. Bad Brad's MO
& since I'm just a lowly temp,

You know HR won't do
A goddamn thing about it—

I'm dying to say (but opt to zip it
For when she's calmer):

Gina, yes I know,
There's still an Everest

Of backlogged rape kits,
But I swear it's a brand new day:

Weinstein's dethroned
& Doctor Huxtable's behind bars

For drugging a legion of women;
Maybe this Me Too movement,

Like a dissident Moses, will lead us all
To the Land of Accountability

& we non-fellating secretaries
& fuckable actors

Can finally tell the Bad Brads of the world
To go take a hike—

.

III. HARUM-SCARUM

FINDING AMERICA IN GOYA'S "BLACK PAINTINGS"

Today, in the Prado's lower gallery, I perceive
Our ailing country's fast-galloping infamy

In Goya's unflinching "Black Paintings."
Our vaunted democracy floundering

Like the Iberian master's sweet, beseeching
Mutt in a quicksand panic,

As Sir Insolvent Mountebank
Runs extravagantly amok—

& how many swastikas & hailstones?
How many catcalls & rapes per hour?—

Through the misted country's spectral atmosphere,
Like Francisco's sooty, scourging colossus—

Meanwhile, in a sorcerer's nocturnal spell,
Señoritas Veracity & Sanity,

Those slandered & jettisoned sisters,
Slowly & fearfully lift, in jeopardy,

From accursed terra firma—hapless
Victims of the genius court painter's

Blood-soaked trio of wing-hatted warlocks
Levitating in a feral frenzy—

LIKE CHRIST OVERTURNING
THE MONEYLENDERS' TABLES

Hard-chasing journalist,
Target in an irascible homeland

That lauds & despises
Your banner of candor & daring

(Uproarious marathon in which
The fiats of neo-cons,

The fluttering of fierce slave-fans,
The steady hiss & malaise

Of fascist foolscap never stops).
Like go-for-broke Christ

In the desecrated temple of the fourth estate,
From outcry to repeated outcry,

Keep ferreting, disclosing, demanding
What's true, dauntless reporter & immanent,

In a time of subterfuge & delusion,
Of unerring rubber bullets

& brutally demolished cameras,
When two & two are tantamount to five,

Keep crying *Geronimo!*
Keep upending the tables.

SENATOR, WHERE IS YOUR VOODOO DOLL, YOUR SNARE?

Decorum won't do the trick;
The price-is-right whores or hallowing intellect.

Match-quick as a vogue-ing mother
From the sassy & treacherous House of LaBeija,

Your irate constituents insist:
Bitch, get real!

Where is your voodoo doll,
Resplendent with pins?

Your tally-ho fox hunter's feisty snare,
Your ready-or-not middle finger?

No more insipid Mother May I,
Insufferable Simon Says,

Or Mother Goose, for God's sakes!
No more beguiling Pied Piper!

Trumpet fanfare
& hearty drumroll, please:

What we need from you,
Posing, slap-on-the-wrist Senator,

Are stratagems beyond your penchant
For ultra-plush accounts,

Elaborate tax dodges & milquetoast assent,
Time & again presenting

America the Beautiful's cherished car keys,
Without a molecule of remorse,

To toadies, phonies & verifiable thieves.
We demand a patriotic love, a prosecution

Whose unsuspected teeth snap shut,
Like a global-warmed polar bear's rictus,

An unapologetic crocodile's jaw,
Like the Big Bad Wolf, nestled

& ready to roll,
In Grandma's frilly nightgown . . .

THE ABSENCE OF THE WITCH DOES NOT INVALIDATE THE SPELL

Mister, from love's keening distance,
I send you dread, discord,

A dead pauper's
Unerring kiss, "double, double,

Toil & trouble"—the foraged
Bolts, welts & buffoonish stitches

Of your own meandering,
Pell-mell Frankenstein;

From Lady Justice's impeccable scales,
I bequeath you

A child's flimsy cootie-catcher,
Opened to the words

Comb-over or *Snake!*—
A throwaway crown, a fake,

Fracked-to-the-hilt
Share of heirloom land,

Acres of unsellable real estate
On the very dissipated earth

You doggedly lacerated
& dismantled—

At an eleventh hour, when the lollygagging,
Wall-building, around-the-clock inanities

& countless renegade cruelties
Have ceased to grow & cascade

Like Rapunzel's hair
& the glittering hourglass sands

Have nearly halted,
Apprentice felon, primetime charlatan,

Un-budging jester on the Hill,
May the emperor-is-naked folderol,

The blight of your slipknot reign,
Your slap-shrill tenure,

Shock your tattered soul in full...

QUID PRO QUO (TWO BARITONES ON A PHONE)

Guess there's been a little change in largesse,
A little hold up, you might call it,

With your country's battle-logged plea
For additional funding.

Frankly, there's zero need at all to include
Mealy-mouth underlings: meddling

"Congresspersons," aggrieved ambassadors,
Or those cloak-&-dagger snitches

Liberals out-&-out praise as whistleblowers;
In heaven's (or Tiger Mother Russia's) name,

It's just between us
Artful & enterprising men:

Two baritones on a phone,
Two stable geniuses—

Hell, it's wartime, Z.,
& you're downright starved

For superior firepower, for buff,
State-of-the-art supplies.

The filthy lowdown is:
I'd like you to slur/ impugn/

Sling bedeviling mud at
A certain polling-high candidate

& his lynchpin,
Paper-pushing son;

Let me be blunt: I'm the Big Daddy
With the dazzling purse strings

& I've got you by
The cowlick/ the coattails/

Your slick ex-Soviet short hairs
(Choose one of the above);

Boy, I'm the badass overseer with the blade
& I've got you hamstrung as a shackled,

Fetched-from-swampland slave
(But what do you eager garlic eaters,

You hinterland guys know
About cotton-picking Dixie field hands anyhow?)

& so my coldcocked marionette,
My Ukrainian cat's-paw,

You do plan to mount & raise
Your fancy victory flag, don't you?

Hmmmmm:
I thought you'd say yes!

HARUM-SCARUM PHOTO OP

In a still reeling, post-slaughter El Paso,
Our Lie-dispensing Sachem grins

& drones like a 5AM newscaster,
Giving the cameraman a discombobulating—

Did I just see that?—thumbs-up,
The very dime store deity

Who spurred a locked-&-loaded
Disciple to declare zealous, all-out war

On "invading" brown people—
In Lady Melania's impeccable Slovenian arms,

Lord have mercy on us,
The infant survivor, gussied up

For this mercilessly lopsided photo op,
In an adorable but reverent

Plaid bow tie, gurgles
& suddenly begins to learn,

In the somersaulting,
Motherless & fatherless world

(Planet the wild-eyed shooter leaves him)
The weight of the word *b-a-w-l*.

THE HOOD

(Abu Ghraib & Vietnam)

O desert corporal,
You of the cardboard pedestal

& scandalous wires,
The dungeon's ink-dark cloth,

Nobody in the instilling army has a clue
You're the very same child

Who stumbled & fumbled to reach
A dilapidated shed,

Failed to fit your first-grade limbs
Into a dingy crawlspace:

All of six—how could you shadow-box
Pterodactyl jungle choppers, grasp

Phantoms of round-eyed
Bar girls in ripped *ao dai?*

You raise a rum-flecked pillow
To ward off the predictable blows

From your dashing,
Dish-breaking,

Back from country Dad
& damned if he doesn't

Scissor the homespun pillowcase
Just to dub you a new Casper—

Little huffing captive
In a funereal cowl,

A lowly chador—
To consign his bullish firstborn,

His little boy hellion,
Back to a claiming darkness:

Here comes the hood in childhood!

THE ONLY WAY TO FIGHT THE PLAGUE IS DECENCY

(an American elegy)

Once upon a time there was a hoax,
A broadcast-to-the-hilt ruse, a puerile

Leader's adamant refusal to rally arms
Against a colossal viral dragon,

A winter hustler's fiat that bloomed,
One titanic, coffin-heavy April,

Into a real-as-your-mama's-dying-hand
Pandemic: national melee, featuring

Stock-selling senators,
Missing-in-action test-kits,

Mask-begging nurses, millionaire high fives
& jerrybuilt morgues,

A storm-haired Lear's flaccid sideshow,
A charlatan's heedless, snake-oil matinee

(Hail the flimflamming functionary
& his red-handed band of rogues).

Land where all the poisonous hierarchies
Arrived to poison us once more—

Where raucous pettiness equaled rollcalling,
Brisk-as-business Death,

Equaled *my crushed kingdom*
For a ventilator!

IV. TANGO WITH A GHOST

OBLITERATE ASYLUM!

Listen, those hometown gangs & death squads
Well, they're fake, *mojado*—

Desecrated hands
& human body parts

The roving killers hang on trees
As a raptor-stern warning—

Remember your sorry country's
Notorious collapse & brisk military coup

Never occurred. Truth to tell,
There's only your impinging lust

For door-opening dollars & fluffy towels,
For shopworn Main Street ideals—

Remember the Tenth Commandment?
Thou shall not covet thy neighbor's _____.

Do you understand? For this,
Your child is torn

From your ignorant & illegal side,
Even from your brown nipple,

For this, you are gassed at the border,
Shunted back to calamity

Or toothless poverty, or detained
At our red-white-&-blue discretion;

About your filthy cage & troubling crime,
Trespasser, invader, let's be frank:

Radiant & glossy, model-svelte
(Think Melania!),

Lady Liberty has a thing to say,
From sea to shining sea:

Obliterate asylum!

REQUIEM FOR ÓSCAR AND VALERIA:
THE CROSSING

In Matamoros, picture it, he wagers the puissant river
That both demurs & caresses,

Promises sanctuary & delivers
The stillness of swift purgatory or heaven—

Óscar Martínez Ramírez fleeing a Salvador
Of reliable vultures & razor-edged threats—refugee,

Too hardscrabble-poor to rustle up
A coyote's preposterous bribe;

Utterly exhausted & adamant to reach
The sanctum of Brownsville, Texas,

Lord, he jumps—
& the Rio Grande's bracing current

Nabs & whisks away the galvanized
Father-in-prayer as he grips his small child—

So in the rending photo,
He's seen luckless, waterborne, bobbing,

His topaz-like girl still
Wrapped in his buffeted, ink-dark tank top—

Don't turn away! We inherited
This sunup-to-sundown dirge, this disavowing,

Impossible border:
Eternally embracing & risk-taking father,

Facedown near the stolid riverbank—

MARTÍN GETSEMANY, I SEE YOU

43 teachers-in-training shunted, eliminated
En route to a rousing march in the capital—

Dauntless Rafael dares me to absorb
His exhibit of all 43 determined faces—believers,

Protestors from the Ayotzinapa Normal School,
So, on the still stinging 5th anniversary of their assassination,

I bring my intent, assessing face
To this underworld sacrilege & roaring,

While Rafael's facial recognition camera
Details my deciphering eyes

& tallied flesh & bone
(How do I breathe with this sudden hush

& surge of quicklime in my chest?)
To discover, with "a level of confidence,"

A match for one of the lost young men:
Martín Getsemany Sánchez García,

You're back from smithereens,
From "burned beyond recognition,"

Promiscuous poppies & cartels,
Day-by-day carrion & cartels,

Throttled strikers & vying gangs,
With Christ's betrayal & plaintive garden

Built right into your compelling name,
With all your young man's ardor & braggadocio—like cologne,

Your uprising beauty & insurgent's wings,
Your deep-set hunger for justice,

To haunt me, Martín Getsemany—*you will die & live*
Under the name of someone

Who has actually died—to nudge
The insensate autumn day

With lime-gloved hands:
You know I dare not look away—

CLARINET

At my family's stained window,
A morning jay.

I stop my scissoring,
As if I could reclaim

A Santiago of bird-call
& sudden ease,

As if I could annul
The battle-gray maze of gutting

Jails, courthouses, morgues—
Purgatory where I bend

Over the burlap,
Again & again,

To show the blunt,
Disillusioning world

The smashed black bell
Of your clarinet.

A blue swatch of your work-shirt becomes
The irrevocable, raw dusk

Of that day;
Here, in this farrago of scraps,

Your living room as I found it:
Lunatic with ripped song sheets…

In imploring red,
A beggar's scuffed vermilion,

I've stitched:
Whoever sees my arpillera,

Help me to pray for my son.
He was seen leaving rehearsal

At 7 o'clock.
He was seen in detention

At Londres #38.
He was seen; he was seen...

After so many years, perhaps
You wouldn't recognize me, Leonel;

I've become the weatherworn,
Undocile woman

Manacled to a tyrant's fence,
A mother dancing the *gueca* solo

In the monitored plaza,
The ache of my make-do arms

Trumpeted,
Your rakish college photo

Pinned to my wind-riffled blouse:
In the *arpillera*,

A tiny, vivid, appliquéd doll,
Forever mourning,

Forever swaying
To your unforgettable woodwind.

TANGO WITH A GHOST

I. Buenos Aires Overture

In a city of bodies shunted
Into clandestine cars—flesh

Hurled from an atavistic chopper's
Staggering height

Into the gagging river,
At vehement wolf's hour

Or sky-staining blue hour,
One body;

In a city, suffused with staunch
Memories of the slandered, the disappeared,

One soul,
One incendiary memory;

In a breeze-swept metropolis
Of numberless phantoms,

A single ghost,
Stubborn as unbridled kudzu

Or all-conquering witch grass;
In a crazy-quilt city

Of come-hither glances
& brazenly expressive limbs,

Pulsing dancehalls & feverish *milongas,*
One impossible tango.

II. *The Living Room Gasp*

That April I was sixteen:
I headed to a local indoor pool,

On a bus full of lanky swimmers,
When my thigh accidentally grazed

The rugged leg of soccer-playing Alejandro,
Exchange student who hailed

From Buenos Aires' refined Retiro district,
After a brief time, I thought I'd faint

From the shock of subterranean pleasure.
A girl-addled junior, I'd never felt

This upending pull
Toward another good-looking boy,

So when I found Alejandro's profile
On a living room mantel shelf in B. A.,

I think I went insane for a time,
Insane:

That Alejandro should return to me
In the scintillating hazel gaze

& undercover hands
Of his strapping nephew Adriano

Was a jack-in-the-box jolt,
An out-of-the-blue mercy—

III. The Vanishing & the Roaring

Adriano, tell me, what happened to your uncle?

My friend, do you know something
About the Dirty War?

You understand,
He simply walked to a student demonstration

On an April night
& never returned.

*

As a necessary history lesson, dapper,
Warm-blooded "Adriano Cool" carts me

To the Casa Rosa,
The presidential palace

Where unfailing mothers of the disappeared
Are still protesting after many years,

So I recall the immense, curved penis
& long, sienna legs of my first *novio*

& in ardent Alejandro's place,
Brusque shouts,

A volley of shots, a roaring:
The castaway limbs of shunted,

Blindfolded students,
Stiff as storefront mannequins in the river.

IV. Tango with a Ghost

"Adriano Cool" whispers:
Amor, if you've had trouble sleeping,

It's because this city, this district
Is so crowded with student ghosts.

*

There's a special tango, A. C. reveals,
Featuring a male dancer, decked

Solely in black, making it seem
Like the lissome woman

Is somehow partnered with a shadow—
Fleet as Hermes, a lord-like shadow

Caresses you; an exhilarating ally
Sparks & shores your tango,

Your fireworks display
Of dancehall skill & ardor:

A lampblack, tantalizing ghost.

*

As if my long-lost soccer prince
Had implored:

Come away with me,
My revenant angel,

From the stark mania of the poisoned river,
The Black Marias,

The harrowing locus of bones:
To strains of masterful Carlos Gardel,

I'll teach you
The most feverish steps.

Buenos Aires is only a burrowing wind,
A sigh, a breeze-swept prayer.

Come dance with me, poet,
In the half-maimed world.

ICEBOX

I. To the Gladiator in the Rogue Arena

Gladiator, whose steely prowess is in service
To a rogue arena,

A sullying Caesar,
With-us-or-against-us strongman,

Confess: are they daunting beasts
In those borderland cages, or children?

Children!
Then go & rescue them from the ruffian world!

II. *Those "Return to Senders" Children*

Separated, the borrowing, the castaway children were blessed with standard American scraps or Chiclets stale cookies wrapped little sweets or hectored, quiet as it's kept, to caress the penises & vulvas of strangers or for their own to be inspected: *Can you keep a secret, Miguel, Maria?* Despite their demerits head lice recalcitrant smell, the border-despising, fundamentally invasive minors were allotted, each to each, their quintessential moment in court, courtesy of almighty Justice, as meted by the greatest country & economy on earth, by the ablest president on the planet. The filth-caked children were, by His gospel & righteous directive, sprayed with a winnowing hose at the sacrosanct border slapped seized tear-gassed caged shunted to ex-internment camps holding pens sally ports forbidden to hug herded under fusty bridges handed with machine-swift severity & clarity to professionals ogres sleepwalkers ill-equipped teens gangs gruff border police ambitious privateers yes even wily traffickers lust-filled clients, maybe over a thousand illegal children—oops!—like so many stamped but still dust-strewn packages the careworn postman mislaid during the bustling Christmas season: *Look, here's a tasty servant-girl-in-training, a surefire ten! Here's a little cherub—a pouty, long-lashed boy, perfect for a secret movie...*

95

III. Icebox

The place where the ensnared children are held
Is sometimes dubbed an "icebox,"

Because of ICE custody, clearly,
But also because

Gelid air is piped, without cease,
Into their fetid cages,

Which must make the baffled kids
Equivalent to frozen peas or chicken;

Yes, chicken is exactly
What some of the boys will become—

IV. The Smithsonian Considers Purchasing the Art
    of Formerly Detained Children

Cages & cyclone fences, chilly underpasses—
What are you saying?

That they don't deserve
Stability or pillows?

Look at the stick figures
Of the once-detained children:

Frowning; frowning again—
Kids shattered,

As sometimes, in the Southern Cone,
In the days of the Dirty War,

To spur "traitorous leftists" to confess,
The fledglings were stripped, demeaned,

Unmade
Right in front of their defiled mothers—

Grief as roaring artifact,
Chaos as cascading history

(Was it your callous voice
Refusing the herded girls

Sanitary napkins, insisting
Let them bleed...)

In those indurate years—
What we did to them,

What we failed to do—
When Betsy Ross's fussed-over stars & stripes,

The United States of Lovingkindness,
Tilted out of the moral universe.

V. Flu Boy Motionless in a Pool

of his own denigrated blood—Guatemalan teen,
Listless, then opossum-stopped, rock-

Still, superfluous beside the toilet bowl
Of his noxious holding cell,

In a lack-love hell
Of chilly concrete & glistening mylar,

Where flu jabs are denied, rescuing
Doctors arrested for presenting serum—

Not a trace of the ash-white ridges
Carlos witnessed on the way,

No warmth of his dreaming cheek
Pressed against the train gondola,

No long-worn rosary,
Nun-blessed & loaned

By his worried *abuelita*,
No milk-tenderness

Of his desperate mother's breast,
No feel of folded, fallback bills

In his dusty pocket,
No discerning nurse

Or scrupulous doctor's gaze
In the nick of time,

No nighttime aegis or active tenderness,
No—

VI. *A Toddler's Day in Court*

Key-cold, the deportation hearing starts,
But now, as if in corrosive homage

To Herr Kafka himself,
The speechless defendant climbs onto the table—

COURAGE SONG FOR SCOTT WARREN

Sing: no more makeshift crosses
In the gangplank desert,

No more "dogcatcher trucks,"
No more jawbones under the moon—

Bring your rebellious grit,
Like a bromide or a borderland candle,

To our bigotry-is-commonplace republic's
Chaos. Bold anima, dissenting angel,

Among the betraying cliffs & dry washes,
The yellow plumes of the *palo verde*,

Be runagate Harriet in a midnight cane field
(General Tubman!), be Martin bravely writing

In an abysmal Birmingham jail.
Yes, your boundless shepherd's gallantry,

Your at-the-ready compassion
Is the rescuing sip

& the heaven-sent gourd required
At all our desperate crossings.

ACKNOWLEDGMENTS

Praise to the Creator for demanding that I speak and pass through great grief, outrage, and annealing fire, in the wake of Mr. Garza's murder, to fashion this book. Thanks to the John Simon Guggenheim Foundation and the Helene B. Wurlitzer Foundation of Taos for generous fellowships, and to Texas State University for a development leave. Let me express my utmost gratitude to Valerie Hegarty for her apt, incredible book cover art. Thanks to Dominic Zuccone for being my close reader this time, to Martín Espada and Ron Slate for supporting this new direction in my work, and to Ilya Kaminsky for publishing a chapbook of the border crisis poems. A thousand thanks to Martha Rhodes and Four Way Books for a double contract!

I can't imagine this project without the abiding legacy of Ai, Federico García Lorca, Audre Lorde, Joni Mitchell, Sylvia Plath, and Adrienne Rich—the artists who first led me to investigate poetry and lyrics in my adolescence. The song "Don't Interrupt the Sorrow" alluded to in "Is Not" is from Mitchell's *The Hissing of Summer Lawns*. Inspired by the ABC series *American Crime,* the dramatic monologue "Boys Don't Do That to Other Boys," is dedicated to Oscar-winning writer-director John Ridley. "The GB Brothers Strike Again," "Me Too, Me Too," and "The Mother Who Says Yes to the Sword" are dedicated to the memory of my former colleague, Ai (1947-2010). "Trafficked Angel" is based, in part, on the testimony of Mexican singer Luis Armando Campos and is dedicated to him. The title "The Absence of The Witch Does Not Invalidate the Spell" is from Emily Dickinson's poem "Long Years apart—can make no..." "The Only Way to Fight the Plague is Decency" is a variation of Dr. Rieux's comment in Camus' 1947 novel *The Plague:* "It may seem a ridiculous idea but the only way to fight the plague is with decency." "Requiem for Óscar and Valeria: The Crossing" is in memory of Óscar Martínez Ramírez and his daughter Valeria, whose bodies were found on the banks of the Rio Grande, June 24, 2019. "Martín Getsemany, I See You" is inspired by Rafael Lozano-Hammer's 2015 art exhibition, "Level of Confidence"; the poem's italicized lines are a sentence from Terrence des Pres' *The Survivor.* "Icebox" was inspired by a reading of Valeria Luiselli's *Tell Me How It Ends.* "Flu Boy Motionless in a Pool" is in memory of sixteen-year-old Carlos Hernández Vásquez, who was found dead on May 20, 2019, in a U. S. Border Patrol holding cell. "Courage Song for Scott Warren" is dedicated to the great border activist who was tried and acquitted three times for his humanitarian aid work.

These poems first appeared in the following magazines and anthologies, some in earlier versions:

American Academy of Poets Poem-A-Day, Borderlands: The Texas Review, The Chicago Quarterly Review, The Cortland Review, The Fight and the Fiddle, Green Mountains Review, The Nervous Breakdown, Nine Mile, On the Seawall, Ploughshares, Poetry International, Poetry Northwest, Solstice: A Magazine of Diverse Voices, The Southampton Review, and *What Saves Us: Poems of Empathy and Outrage in the Age of Trump* (Northwestern University Press).

Cyrus Cassells is the 2021 Poet Laureate of Texas. Among his honors: a Guggenheim fellowship, the National Poetry Series, a Lambda Literary Award, a Lannan Literary Award, two NEA grants, a Pushcart Prize, and the William Carlos Williams Award. His 2018 volume, *The Gospel according to Wild Indigo,* was a finalist for the NAACP Image Award, the Helen C. Smith Memorial Award, and the Balcones Poetry Prize. *Still Life with Children: Selected Poems of Francesc Parcerisas*, translated from the Catalan, was awarded the Texas Institute of Letters' Soeurette Diehl Fraser Award for Best Translated Book of 2018 and 2019. He was nominated for the 2019 Pulitzer Prize in Criticism for his film and television reviews in *The Washington Spectator*. He teaches in the M. F. A. program at Texas State University and is the recipient of the 2021 Presidential Award for Scholarly/Creative Activities, one of the university's highest honors.

Publication of this book was made possible by grants and donations. We are also grateful to those individuals who participated in our 2021 Build a Book Program. They are:

Anonymous (16), Maggie Anderson, Susan Kay Anderson, Kristina Andersson, Kate Angus, Kathy Aponick, Sarah Audsley, Jean Ball, Sally Ball, Clayre Benzadón, Greg Blaine, Laurel Blossom, Adam Bohannon, Betsy Bonner, Lee Briccetti, Joan Bright, Jane Martha Brox, Susan Buttenwieser, Anthony Cappo, Carla and Steven Carlson, Paul and Brandy Carlson, Renee Carlson, Alice Christian, Karen Rhodes Clarke, Mari Coates, Jane Cooper, Ellen Cosgrove, Peter Coyote, Robin Davidson, Kwame Dawes, Michael Anna de Armas, Brian Komei Dempster, Renko and Stuart Dempster, Matthew DeNichilo, Rosalynde Vas Dias, Kent Dixon, Patrick Donnelly, Lynn Emanuel, Blas Falconer, Elliot Figman, Jennifer Franklin, Helen Fremont and Donna Thagard, Gabriel Fried, John Gallaher, Reginald Gibbons, Jason Gifford, Jean and Jay Glassman, Dorothy Tapper Goldman, Sarah Gorham and Jeffrey Skinner, Lauri Grossman, Julia Guez, Sarah Gund, Naomi Guttman and Jonathan Mead, Kimiko Hahn, Mary Stewart Hammond, Beth Harrison, Jeffrey Harrison, Melanie S. Hatter, Tom Healy and Fred Hochberg, K.T. Herr, Karen Hildebrand, Joel Hinman, Deming Holleran, Lillian Howan, Thomas and Autumn Howard, Catherine Hoyser, Elizabeth Jackson, Jessica Jacobs and Nickole Brown, Christopher Johanson, Jen Just, Maeve Kinkead, Alexandra Knox, Lindsay and John Landes, Suzanne Langlois, Laura Lauth, Sydney Lea, David Lee and Jamila Trindle, Rodney Terich Leonard, Jen Levitt, Howard Levy, Owen Lewis, Matthew Lippman, Jennifer Litt, Karen Llagas, Sara London and Dean Albarelli, Clarissa Long, James Longenbach, Cynthia Lowen, Ralph and Mary Ann Lowen, Ricardo Maldonado, Myra Malkin, Jacquelyn Malone, Carrie Mar, Kathleen McCoy, Ellen McCulloch-Lovell, Lupe Mendez, David Miller, Josephine Miller, Nicki Moore, Guna Mundheim, Matthew Murphy and Maura Rockcastle, Michael and Nancy Murphy, Myra Natter, Jay Baron Nicorvo, Ashley Nissler, Kimberly Nunes, Rebecca and Daniel Okrent, Robert Oldshue and Nina Calabresi, Kathleen Ossip,

Judith Pacht, Cathy McArthur Palermo, Marcia and Chris Pelletiere, Sam Perkins, Susan Peters and Morgan Driscoll, Patrick Phillips, Robert Pinsky, Megan Pinto, Connie Post, Kyle Potvin, Grace Prasad, Kevin Prufer, Alicia Jo Rabins, Anna Duke Reach, Victoria Redel, Martha Rhodes, Paula Rhodes, Louise Riemer, Sarah Santner, Amy Schiffman, Peter and Jill Schireson, Roni and Richard Schotter, James and Nancy Shalek, Soraya Shalforoosh, Peggy Shinner, Anita Soos, Donna Spruijt-Metz, Ann F. Stanford, Arlene Stang, Page Hill Starzinger, Marina Stuart, Yerra Sugarman, Marjorie and Lew Tesser, Eleanor Thomas, Tom Thompson and Miranda Field, James Tjoa, Ellen Bryant Voigt, Connie Voisine, Moira Walsh, Ellen Dore Watson, Calvin Wei, John Wender, Eleanor Wilner, Mary Wolf, and Pamela and Kelly Yenser.